The Joy of Bo

A smarter way to learn the most popular front-end ⌐work for developing responsive, mobile first projects on the web.

by

Alan Forbes

http://www.joyofbootstrap.com

The Joy of Bootstrap

Table of Contents

What is Bootstrap?

Introduction

Bootstrap is a free collection of tools for creating awesome websites and web applications. It contains HTML and CSS-based design templates for typography, forms, buttons, navigation and other interface components such as menus, headers, and image carousels.

Bootstrap started off as an internal project at Twitter but the guys who built it (Mark Otto and Jacob Thornton) got management approval to open source it. For this reason, Bootstrap is sometimes also referred to as 'Twitter Bootstrap'.

One of the great things about Bootstrap is that it is designed to be "mobile first". This means that the things you build with Bootstrap to look great on a regular browser will also (generally) look great on a mobile device too without any extra work. By 'mobile device' I mean a gadget with a small screen factor, such as smart phone. Bootstrap is **responsive**.

Responsive means that your page will respond to different sized screens by automatically adjusting its layout to look good.

Even better, working with Bootstrap is just *plain fun* too. That's what inspired me to write this book-- so you could have fun with Bootstrap too.

Let's get started.

Where to get Bootstrap

There are two ways to start using Bootstrap on your web site. You can:

1. Download the Bootstrap library from getBootstrap.com or,

2. Include Bootstrap from a CDN

Downloading Bootstrap

There are three versions of Bootstrap available for downloading: 1) the compiled and minified version which contains the CSS, JavaScript, and fonts, but not documentation or source files, 2) The source code version which contains the source Less, JavaScript, font files, and documentation, and 3) and the SAAS version which is Bootstrap ported from Less to Sass for inclusion in Rails, Compass, or Sass-only projects.

Unless you are looking to tinker with the underlying structure of Bootstrap, you should probably go for option one-- the compiled and minified version.

But then again, you don't even need to download Bootstrap to use it. You could just use the hosted version.

Hosted Bootstrap

A company called MaxCDN is hosting Bootstrap. It is a good idea to check the MaxCDN website to get the latest links, which you can do at http://www.bootstrapcdn.com/.   As of the writing of this book, to use Bootstrap MaxCDN just include the the following code on your page:

Max CDN:

```
<head>
<!-- Latest compiled and minified CSS -->
<link rel="stylesheet"
href="//netdna.bootstrapcdn.com/bootstrap/3.1.1/css/bootstrap.min.css">

<!-- Optional theme -->
<link rel="stylesheet"
href="//netdna.bootstrapcdn.com/bootstrap/3.1.1/css/bootstrap-
theme.min.css">

<!-- Latest compiled and minified JavaScript -->
<script
src="//netdna.bootstrapcdn.com/bootstrap/3.1.1/js/bootstrap.min.js"></scrip
t>
</script>
</head>
```

Using a hosted version of Bootstrap has some advantages over hosting it yourself. Many users will have already downloaded Bootstrap when visiting a different site. As a result, they won't need to download it again because their browser will already have it stored locally. This leads to faster loading time of your site. Also, most CDN's will make sure that when a user requests a file it will be served from the server closest to them, which may well be closer (and more importantly faster) than your server.

> Unless you have a compelling reason to host Bootstrap yourself, you should use a CDN (Content Delivery Network).

Potential Gotcha!

Note that if you use the style shown above to refer to the hosted Bootstrap, such as href="//netdna.bootstrapcdn.com... then the URL used to retrieve the CSS will use the same protocol as the page in which it is hosted. In other words, if your page is on http://www.joyofbootstrap which uses the http protocol, then it will connect to netdna.bootstrapcdn.com using http as well.

If your page is on a secure server using https, then Bootstrap will come using https. Likewise if it is on a regular (non-secure) http server, then Bootstrap will use http when it evaluates how to get to **//netdna.boostrapcdn.com**.

This means that if you copy some of the source code from the book to your local machine and then just open it in a browser it will use the **file protocol** to try to get the Bootstrap files, which won't work.

Basic Text Coloring

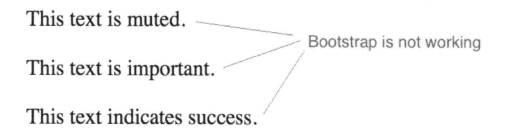

It doesn't work because it tries to get the Bootstrap css from your local file system, using the path specified.

The solution, if you need to view files locally, is to either 1) write out the entire url including the protocol, such as

```
<link href="http://maxcdn.bootstrapcdn.com/bootstrap/3.1.1/css/bootstrap.min.css"
rel="stylesheet">
```

or, 2) copy Bootstrap to your file system and then modify the href path to the location where the file actually exists. Note that if you move this to a server at some point, you'll need to duplicate the path on the server to match that of your local machine.

Here's the exact same file, with no change at all, running on a server. In this case, the hosted Bootstrap is retrieved using http, which is *implied* protocol.

The file works because the Bootstrap CDN can be retrieved using HTTP.

> Annoyingly for us, but in an attempt to make browsers simpler for the masses, most browsers now hide the protocol (such as http://) when displaying URLs in the address bar.

LESS

Bootstrap is modular and consists essentially of a series of <u>LESS stylesheets</u> that implement the various components of the toolkit. A stylesheet called bootstrap.less includes the components stylesheets. You probably have never heard of LESS; at least I hadn't heard of it until I discovered Bootstrap.

> **LESS** (Leaner CSS) is a dynamic stylesheet *language* which outputs standard CSS files.

LESS is a language that makes the maintenance of complex stylesheets easier. You do **not** have to understand LESS to make use of Bootstrap. You do have to understand it if you want to seriously customize Bootstrap though.

Here's a very short introduction to LESS. LESS allows variables to be defined which are substituted for CSS when the file is translated. LESS variables are defined with an at sign(@). Variable assignment is done with a colon (:).

During translation, the values of the variables are inserted into the output CSS document.

```
@color: #4D926F;

#header {
  color: @color;
}
h2 {
  color: @color;
}
```

The code above in LESS would compile to the following CSS code.

```
#header {
  color: #4D926F;
}
h2 {
  color: #4D926F;
}
```

As you can imagine, creating stylesheets this way has some advantages because when you want to change a color, for instance, you don't have to change it in a million places-- you only have to change the value of the variable. There is much more to LESS than this. You can even write functions that evaluate into CSS, but this is beyond the scope of this book.

2

Getting Started with Bootstrap

HTML5 doctype

Bootstrap makes use of certain HTML elements and CSS properties that require the use of the HTML5 doctype. Include it at the beginning of **all** your projects.

```
<!DOCTYPE html>
<html lang="en">
  ...
</html>
```

Mobile first

Starting with Bootstrap 3, the entire project is designed to be responsive to mobile devices. Instead of having to remember to include optional mobile styles, they're already part of the core framework. In fact, Bootstrap is automatically responsive to different sized screens.

To ensure proper rendering and touch zooming, **add the viewport meta tag to your** <head>.

```
<meta name="viewport" content="width=device-width, initial-scale=1">
```

You can disable zooming capabilities on mobile devices by adding user-

`scalable=no` to the viewport meta tag. This disables zooming, meaning users are only able to scroll, and results in your site feeling a bit more like a native application, but understand that users might find the fact that they can't zoom annoying.

```
<meta name="viewport" content="width=device-width, initial-scale=1,
maximum-scale=1, user-scalable=no">
```

Typography and links

Bootstrap sets basic global display, typography, and link styles. This is covered in more detail in Chapter 6: Typography, but to give you a quic overview Bootstrap by default will:

- Set `background-color: #fff;` on the `body`

- Use the `@font-family-base`, `@font-size-base`, and `@line-height-base` attributes as the typographic base

- Set the global link color via `@link-color` and apply link underlines only on `:hover`

These styles can be found (and modified) within `scaffolding.less`.

Containers

Easily center a page's contents by wrapping its contents in a `.container`. Containers set `width` at various media query breakpoints to match our grid system.

Note that containers are not nestable. This means you cannot put a container inside another container. You are limited to one per page.

```
<div class="container">
  ...
</div>
```

Basic Bootstrap Page

It doesn't take much to add Bootstrap to your page. Here's a basic page with all the elements required to use Bootstrap.

```html
<!DOCTYPE html>
<html lang="en">
 <head>
  <meta name="viewport" content="width=device-width, initial-scale=1">
  <title>Bootstrap 101 Template</title>

  <!-- Bootstrap -->
  <!-- Latest compiled and minified CSS -->
  <link rel="stylesheet"
href="//netdna.bootstrapcdn.com/bootstrap/3.1.1/css/bootstrap.min.cs
s">

  <!-- Optional theme -->
  <link rel="stylesheet"
href="//netdna.bootstrapcdn.com/bootstrap/3.1.1/css/bootstrap-
theme.min.css">

 </head>
 <body>
  <h1>Hello, world!</h1>

  <!-- jQuery (necessary for Bootstrap's JavaScript plugins) -->
  <script
src="https://ajax.googleapis.com/ajax/libs/jquery/1.11.0/jquery.min.
js"></script>
  <!-- Include all compiled plugins (below), or include individual files as
needed -->
  <!-- Latest compiled and minified JavaScript -->
  <script
src="//netdna.bootstrapcdn.com/bootstrap/3.1.1/js/bootstrap.min.js">
</script>
 </body>
</html>
```

Bootstrap is Themable

One of the things about Bootstrap is that is very easy to change the look and feel of Bootstrap by applying a new theme to it.

One great place to get Bootstrap themes for free is the website:

http://bootswatch.com

If you don't mind paying a little for something awesome, I also like this site:

https://wrapbootstrap.com

3

Source Code and Sample Website

Introduction

I've found that one of the best ways to learn something is to be able to apply it right away in a realistic context. Toward that end, I'm providing two different ways for you to learn by doing as we go along through this book.

First, I'm providing a sample website for a fictional company called "Sam's Used Cars". It starts as an HTML only website, and we'll enhance it a bit with each chapter so you can see the effect of Bootstrap on a real site.

Second, the http://www.JoyofBootstrap.com website contains dozens of examples from the book and features an innovative "See Code" editor which lets you experiment with the code and see the results immediately.

I strongly urge you to use **both** resources.

Sam's Used Cars

If you've read either of my previous books, The Joy of PHP or The Joy of jQuery, you may be familiar with Sam already.

Sam runs a used car dealership that started off small but grew over time. As his business grew, the needs of his website grew as well. When you only have 4 or 5 cars for sale at a time, manually modifying your website as one car is sold and thus no longer available or adding a new one that you just added to the sales lot in hopes of selling is not too much work.   But as your inventory grows from 5 cars to 10 cars, and then again to 20 cars or more the effort required to keep the website up to date can quickly become a full time position.

This is where The *Joy of PHP* comes in. We transformed Sam's HTML website where every page was hand coded into one that is created dynamically using PHP. The information about the cars is stored in a mySQL database and is always up to date.   All Sam has to do now is keep his mySQL database up to date by filling out web forms describing the new cars and deleting rows for cars that have already been sold.

We're going to do the same thing with this book. We'll start of with Sam's HTML-only web site which looks terrible on mobile devices and gradually transform it into something that is fully Bootstrap enabled and awesome.

Source Code on JoyofBootstrap.com

Another important part of learning is playing. You can get all the source code that accompanies this book by visiting http://www.JoyofBootstrap.com.

The site is set up so you can see the examples in action (click the link '**See Code**' that accompanies every example) and even **tweak** the source code online and see the results of your changes without having to download or install anything.

Every chapter has a number of examples online associated with it. Don't move to the next chapter until you have tried the examples either online or on your own computer.   It's really the only way to truly get it.

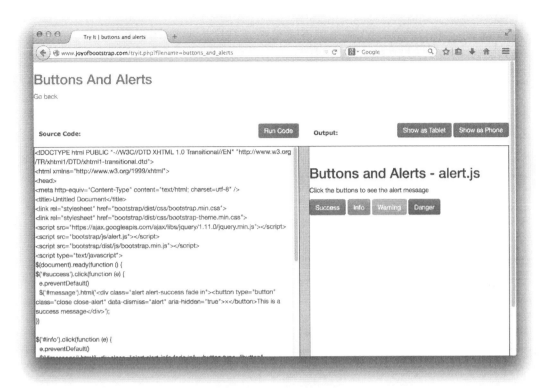

Illustration 1: www.joyofbootstrap.com web site

I also invite you to join my mailing list. I'll never spam you, and you can always opt out if you lose interest. Although I haven't done any yet, I do intent to make some youtube videos of the source code in action and I'll update everyone on the mailing list as they come out. Examples with a video will have a 'play video' button.

Contacting the Author

I invite you to contact me if you have any book feedback (such as typos or code bugs) or questions. If there's something you just don't get, maybe other people will have the same issue and it means I need to improve that particular section. I take the time to get back to everyone who emails me. I'm at AlanForbes@outlook.com

Installing for a Web Site

If you want to make the application you've built to be available to everybody via the Internet, you'll need to install your application onto a publicly accessible server.   Typically that means finding a hosting provider.

If you are looking for an inexpensive hosting provider, I use AccuWeb Hosting for www.joyofbootstrap.com, and I haven't had any problems with them. If you'd like to use them too, I would appreciate if you use my affiliate link at https://manage.accuwebhosting.com/aff.php?aff=743

Using the above link won't cost you any more, and (in theory) I'll get a small commission on the sale. Thank you.

4

The Grid System

Introduction

One of the particularly cool features of Bootstrap is it's ability to resize automatically for different size devices. On a big screen you might have content organized into multiple columns, but on a small screen it would make more sense for the content items to be stacked on top of each other.

This is easily accomplished using Bootstrap's grid system. Bootstrap's grid system allows you to have up to 12 columns across the page. Basically the way that it works is to imagine the screen divided into 12 equal units. If you don't want to use all 12 units individually, you can group some of the units together to form wider columns.

For instance to have three columns across a page you would have three groups of four units each. If you want your content spread across two columns, set it up as two groups of six units each.   The columns do not have to be equal, but the total number of units used needs to add up to twelve.

But here is the cool part: Bootstrap is able to tell what size the screen is, and rearrange the columns accordingly.

When you set up your columns, you assign them a class. The class **suffix** tells Bootstrap how many units to consume. For instance, the class .col-sm-6 will tell Bootstrap to use 6 units.   Six is the suffix.

The class prefix tells Bootstrap on which sized screens you would like this column to appear. The possible prefixes are:

.col-xs- for extra small devices, such as phones (<768px)

.col-sm- for small devices, such as tablets (≥768px)

.col-md- for medium devices, such as laptops (≥992px)

.col-lg- for large devices, such as computers with external monitors (≥1200px)

The prefix you use means that the column will be shown as a separate column on devices this size **and larger.**   Hopefully an example will make this clear. If you set two columns using the .col-md-6 class, you will see two columns on medium and higher devices, but the columns will be stacked on top of each other for tablets and phones.

The code for that would look like this:

```
<div class="row">
  <div class="col-md-1">.col-md-1</div>
  <div class="col-md-1">.col-md-1</div>
  <div class="col-md-1">.col-md-1</div>
  <div class="col-md-1">.col-md-1</div>
  <div class="col-md-1">.col-md-1</div>
  <div class="col-md-1">.col-md-1</div>
  <div class="col-md-1">.col-md-1</div>
  <div class="col-md-1">.col-md-1</div>
  <div class="col-md-1">.col-md-1</div>
  <div class="col-md-1">.col-md-1</div>
  <div class="col-md-1">.col-md-1</div>
  <div class="col-md-1">.col-md-1</div>
</div>
```

To create two unequal columns, one 8 units wide and one 4 units wide, the following code would apply:

```
<div class="row">
  <div class="col-md-8">.col-md-8</div>
  <div class="col-md-4">.col-md-4</div>
</div>
```

To create three equal columns, the following code would apply:

```
<div class="row">
  <div class="col-md-4">.col-md-4</div>
  <div class="col-md-4">.col-md-4</div>
  <div class="col-md-4">.col-md-4</div>
</div>
```

To create two equal columns, the following code would apply:

```
<div class="row">
  <div class="col-md-6">.col-md-6</div>
  <div class="col-md-6">.col-md-6</div>
</div>
```

There is an example of this code on the http://www.joyofbootstrap.com website, titled 'Basic Grid System'.

Beyond Simple Stacking

You can also give columns multiple classes, so that they behave differently on different sized devices. In other words, stack on small devices, split to two columns on medium devices, and spread across four columns on full-sized screens.

```
<!-- Stack the columns on mobile by making one full-width and the
other half-width -->
<div class="row">
  <div class="col-xs-12 col-md-8">.col-xs-12 .col-md-8</div>
  <div class="col-xs-6 col-md-4">.col-xs-6 .col-md-4</div>
</div>

<!-- Columns start at 50% wide on mobile and bump up to 33.3% wide
on desktop -->
<div class="row">
  <div class="col-xs-6 col-md-4">.col-xs-6 .col-md-4</div>
  <div class="col-xs-6 col-md-4">.col-xs-6 .col-md-4</div>
  <div class="col-xs-6 col-md-4">.col-xs-6 .col-md-4</div>
</div>

<!-- Columns are always 50% wide, on mobile and desktop -->
<div class="row">
  <div class="col-xs-6">.col-xs-6</div>
  <div class="col-xs-6">.col-xs-6</div>
</div>
```

There is an example of this code on the http://www.joyofbootstrap.com website, titled *'Grid For Mobile And Desktop'.*

5

Glyphicons

Introduction

Glyphicons are icons you can use to make your page more interesting looking. You can put in an icon just about anywhere by using the following syntax.

```
<span class="glyphicon glyphicon-name"></span>
```

Where you substitute the text **glyphicon-name** with the name of actual icon you want to use, for instance:

```
<span class="glyphicon glyphicon-info-sign"></span>
```

Glyphicons can also be used inside buttons

```
<button type="button" class="btn btn-default btn-lg">
  <span class="glyphicon glyphicon-star"></span> Star
</button>
```

Simple Glyphicon Code Example

```html
<!DOCTYPE html>
<html lang="en">
<head>
<meta http-equiv="Content-Type" content="text/html; charset=utf-8" />
<title></title>
<link rel="stylesheet" href="bootstrap/dist/css/bootstrap.min.css">
<link rel="stylesheet" href="bootstrap/dist/css/bootstrap-
theme.min.css">
 <script
src="https://ajax.googleapis.com/ajax/libs/jquery/1.11.0/jquery.min.
js"></script>
<script src="bootstrap/dist/js/bootstrap.min.js"></script>

</head>
 <body>
<div class="container">
<h2>Basic Glyphicon</h2>
<p>Would you like to <span class="glyphicon glyphicon-search"></span>
search for something?</p>
<p>Perhaps you would like to make me your favorite?</p>
<button type="button" class="btn btn-default btn-lg">
 <span class="glyphicon glyphicon-star"></span> Star
</button>

 </div>
 </body>
</html>
```

There is an example of this code on the http://www.joyofbootstrap.com website, titled *'Using Glyphicons'.*

All Available Glyphicons

You can see a list of all the available Glyphicons and how they were created by looking at the example of this code on the http://www.joyofbootstrap.com website, titled *'List Of Available Glyphicons'*.

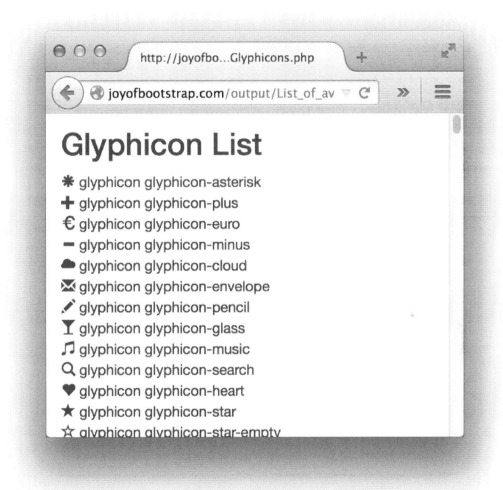

Tables

Introduction

Bootstrap's primary purpose is to make your web pages look great. Tables are a very common element on web pages and Bootstrap can make your tables look great too.

Basic Table example

For basic styling—light padding and only horizontal dividers—add the base class `.table` to any `<table>`. It may seem redundant to do that, but given the widespread use of tables for other plugins like calendars and date pickers, the Bootstrap team opted to isolate their custom table styles to those tables which you want the styles applied.

```
<table class="table">
  ...
</table>
```

There is an example of this code on the http://www.joyofbootstrap.com website, titled *'Table'*.

Striped rows

Use `.table-striped` to add zebra-striping to any table.

```
<table class="table table-striped">
  ...
</table>
```

This doesn't work with IE 8, because Striped tables are styled via the `:nth-child` CSS selector, which is not available in Internet Explorer 8.

Bordered table

Add `.table-bordered` for borders on all sides of the table and cells.

```
<table class="table table-bordered">
  ...
</table>
```

Hover rows

Add `.table-hover` to enable a hover state on table rows within a `<tbody>`.

```
<table class="table table-hover">
  ...
</table>
```

Condensed table

Add `.table-condensed` to make tables more compact by cutting cell padding in half.

```
<table class="table table-condensed">
  ...
</table>
```

Contextual classes

Contextual classes is a fancy way to say that you want to give a row some kind of context. In other words, to make a particular row stand out for one reason or another.

Contextual classes allow you to color table rows or individual cells.

.active – Applies the hover color to a particular row or cell

.success – Indicates a successful or positive action

.info – Indicates a neutral informative change or action

.warning – Indicates a warning that might need attention

.danger – Indicates a dangerous or potentially negative action

Contextual classes can be applied to table rows or to table cells.

Using Contextual Classes on Table Rows

```
<!-- On rows -->
<tr class="active">...</tr>
<tr class="success">...</tr>
<tr class="warning">...</tr>
<tr class="danger">...</tr>
<tr class="info">...</tr>
```

Using Contextual Classes on Table Cells

```
<!-- On cells (`td` or `th`) -->
<tr>
  <td class="active">...</td>
  <td class="success">...</td>
  <td class="warning">...</td>
  <td class="danger">...</td>
  <td class="info">...</td>
</tr>
```

There is a great example of a variety of tables on the
http://www.joyofbootstrap.com website, titled *'Advanced Table Formatting'*.

7

Typography

Introduction

Bootstrap can make a mediocre page look great almost without any effort. The Bootstrap CSS automatically applies to common HTML elements.

Headings

All HTML headings, `<h1>` through `<h6>` are automatically styled. There are also `h1` through `h6` classes that can be assigned to paragraphs and spans for when you want to match the font styling of a heading but still want your text to be displayed inline.

```
<h2>heading two</h2>
<p class='h2'>This is a test</p>
<p>This is <span class='h3'>also</span> a test</p>
```

Create lighter, secondary text within a heading by using the `<small>` tag or the `small` class.

```
<h1>Bootstrap heading <small>Secondary text</small></h1>
```

If you don't do anything at all to a paragraph, then the Bootstraps defaults will apply. Bootstrap's global default `font-size` is **14px**, with a `line-height` of **1.428**. This is applied to the `<body>` and all paragraphs. In addition, `<p>`

(paragraphs) receive a bottom margin of half their computed line-height (10px by default).

```
<p>...</p>
```

Lead body copy

You can make a paragraph stand out by adding the class "lead" to the paragraph tag. Generally, you would only do this to one paragraph, near the top of the page.

```
<p class="lead">Here's the attention grabber</p>
```

Block Quotes

You can make a quote stand out by using the class "blockquote" to the paragraph tag. If you want the quote on the right, add class="pull-right",

```
<blockquote>If you think you have problems with math, you should see
my problems.<small>Albert Einstein, <cite title="Source
Title">Physicist</cite></small></blockquote>
```

If you think you have problems with math, you should see my problems.
— Albert Einstein, Physicist

There is a great example of a variety of tables on the http://www.joyofbootstrap.com website, titled *'Block Quote'*.

Contextual colors

Convey meaning through color with a handful of emphasis utility classes. These may also be applied to links and will darken on hover just like other default link styles.

```
<p class="text-muted">This text is muted.</p>
<p class="text-primary">This text is important.</p>
<p class="text-success">This text indicates success.</p>
<p class="text-info">This text is used to convey information.</p>
<p class="text-warning">This text is used to convey a warning.</p>
<p class="text-danger">This text is used to convey danger.</p>
```

Dealing with specific cases

Sometimes the emphasis classes cannot be applied because another selector is taking over. In most cases, you can get around this by wrapping your text in a `<span>` with the desired class.

```
<p>This is a <span class='text-danger'>dangerous</span> situation.</p>
```

Contextual backgrounds

Similar to the contextual **text** color classes, you can also easily set the **background** of an element to any contextual class. Anchor components will darken on hover, just like the text classes.

```
<p class="bg-primary">...</p>
<p class="bg-success">...</p>
<p class="bg-info">...</p>
<p class="bg-warning">...</p>
<p class="bg-danger">...</p>
```

There is a great example of a variety of tables on the http://www.joyofbootstrap.com website, titled *'Emphasis Classes'*

Built with Less

The typographic scale used throughout Bootstrap is based on two Less variables which can be found in the **variables.less** file: `@font-size-base` and `@line-height-base`. The first is the base font-size used throughout and the second is the base line-height. These values are the basis for the margins, paddings, and line-heights of all the Bootstrap CSS.

That's the power of Less – rather than hard-coding specific values for margins and paddings these things can be calculated in proportion to some base values.

Customize `@font-size-base` and `@line-height-base` and Bootstrap adapts accordingly.

Sam's Used Cars Challenge

See if you can apply the typography features described in this chapter to Sam's Used Cars website. When you're done, the home page should feature some catchy text, which *might* look something like this:

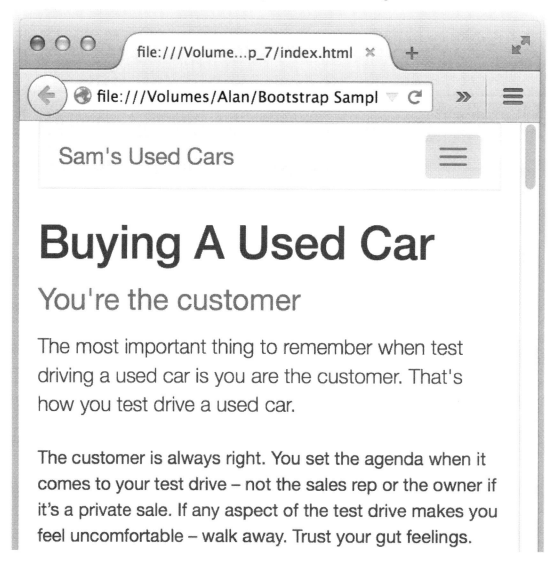

Challenge Solution

Of course, use your own creativity to come up with how you would set up the site if you were Sam.

One possible solution can be found in the example file Sams_Used_Cars_Chap_7.zip

8

Making a Page Responsive

Introduction

Big part of the value proposition of bootstrap is the fact that it makes pages respond automatically to different sized screens. This does not happen automatically, though.

While Bootstrap makes it easy, you still do have *some* work to do. There are some great classes which can be used to selective hide or show specific elements depending on the screen size.   These include visible-xs to visible-lg and hidden-xs to hidden-lg.

	Extra small devices Phones (<768px)	Small devices Tablets (≥768px)	Medium devices Desktops (≥992px)	Large devices Desktops (≥1200px)
.visible-xs	Visible	Hidden	Hidden	Hidden
.visible-sm	Hidden	Visible	Hidden	Hidden
.visible-md	Hidden	Hidden	Visible	Hidden
.visible-lg	Hidden	Hidden	Hidden	Visible
.hidden-xs	Hidden	Visible	Visible	Visible
.hidden-sm	Visible	Hidden	Visible	Visible
.hidden-md	Visible	Visible	Hidden	Visible
.hidden-lg	Visible	Visible	Visible	Hidden

A

An item marked with one of the **visible** tags will only be visible on the specified screen size while an item marked with the **hidden** classes will be hidden on that sized screen.

```
<div class="container">
<h2>Responsiveness</h2>
<p class='hidden-lg'>This is hidden on large screens, visible on others.</p>
<p class='hidden-sm'>This is hidden on small screens, but visible on others.</p>
<p class='visible-md'>This is visible on medium screens, but invisible on others.</p>
  </div>
```

There is an example of technique on the http://www.joyofbootstrap.com website, titled 'Responsiveness'.

Responsive tables

Create responsive tables by surrounding the table which is using the **table** class (<table class="table">) with a div tag using the **table-responsive** class, as shown below:

```
<div class="table-responsive">
 <table class="table">

   ...
 </table>
</div>
```

This will make the table scroll horizontally up to small devices (under 768px). When viewing on anything larger than 768px wide, you will not see any difference in these tables.

9

Dropdowns and Nav Bars

Introduction

Navigation refers to helping people find their way around your website. This can mean menus, tables, links, breadcrumbs and more. Ideally, you have *just enough* navigational aids to help your visitor find their way around without overdoing it.

One of the challenges is displaying the appropriate navigation for the device viewing the page. On a large screen, a full menu of options might be appropriate but that same page viewed on a phone or tablet might leave room for little else. Bootstrap is great for solving this common problem.

The Nav Bar

Bootstrap's Navbars are **responsive** components that serve as navigation headers for your application or site. When viewed on a small screen they collapse automatically, as shown below. To see the menu one has to click the icon on the right:

As the screen gets larger the navbar will extend across the screen, and hide the icon, as shown:

Sam's Used Cars   Home   About   Services   Galleries   Contact

Examples

You can try out (and even change) some examples of Navigation on the http://www.joyofbootstrap.com website.

Drop Downs

A drop down is a user interface element that is supposed to stay mostly out of the way. Most menus are implemented as drop downs, meaning that the categories are visible and if you click on a category the items in the category then "drop down" and become visible.

Shown below is the menu for Outlook.com mail. Some items are action buttons and others reveal menus when you click on them. The menu you can see is called the Nav bar and the items that appear only when you click on them are the drop downs.

Reply | ⌄   Delete   Archive   Junk | ⌄   Sweep   Move to ⌄

A user interface convention that seems to have become somewhat expected is to use the down arrow character (shown to the right of Reply and Junk) to indicate a drop down. This can be done in Bootstrap in one of two ways:

1. <span class="caret"></span>

2. `<span class="glyphicon glyphicon-chevron-down"></span>`

Since the first way is shorter, that's generally what I use.

Drop Downs require jQuery

Because a drop down menu is not just static text on a screen but actually interactive, a bit of jQuery is required to get them to work. Luckily this is pretty standard:

```
<script>
$(document).ready(function(){
    $(window).scroll(function () {
        if ($(this).scrollTop() > 50) {
            $('#back-to-top').fadeIn();
        } else {
            $('#back-to-top').fadeOut();
        }
    });
    // scroll body to 0px on click
    $('#back-to-top').click(function () {
        $('#back-to-top').tooltip('hide');
        $('body,html').animate({
            scrollTop: 0
        }, 800);
        return false;
    });

    $('#back-to-top').tooltip('show');

});
</script>
<style>
.back-to-top {
    cursor: pointer;
    position: fixed;
    bottom: 30px;
    right:30px;
    display:none;
}
</style>
```

Sample Code

Here's an example of a complete drop down. You can try out this example on the http://www.joyofbootstrap.com website, titled 'Drop Down on Hover'.

```html
<!DOCTYPE html>
<html lang="en">
<head>
<meta http-equiv="Content-Type" content="text/html; charset=utf-8" />
<title></title>
<link rel="stylesheet" href="bootstrap/dist/css/bootstrap.min.css">
<link rel="stylesheet" href="bootstrap/dist/css/bootstrap-theme.min.css">
   <script src="https://ajax.googleapis.com/ajax/libs/jquery/1.11.0/jquery.min.js"></script>
<script src="bootstrap/dist/js/bootstrap.min.js"></script>
<style>
.show-on-hover:hover > ul.dropdown-menu {
   display: block;
}
</style>
</head>
<body>

<div class="container">
<div class="btn-group show-on-hover">
      <button type="button" class="btn btn-default dropdown-toggle" data-toggle="dropdown">
      Action <span class="caret"></span>
      </button>
      <ul class="dropdown-menu" role="menu">
       <li><a href="#">Action</a></li>
       <li><a href="#">Another action</a></li>
       <li><a href="#">Something else here</a></li>
       <li class="divider"></li>
       <li><a href="#">Separated link</a></li>
      </ul>
    </div>
</div>
</body>
</html>
```

Sam's Used Cars Challenge

See if you can apply the feature described in this chapter to Sam's Used Cars website.

When you're done, the menu across the top should look something like this:

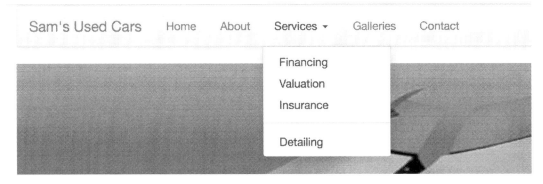

Challenge Solution

Of course, use your own creativity to come up with how you would set up the menu if you were Sam.

One possible solution can be found in the example file Sams_Used_Cars_Chap_09.zip

Bonus Round

If you want to take it even further experiment with Bootstrap themes to make it a little more colorful. Even I think the gray theme is **boring**.

10

Buttons

Introduction

Bootstrap provides seven styles (more accurately, classes) of buttons. To style a button using Bootstrap just add the class **btn** followed by the style, such as **btn-primary,** (class="btn btn-primary"), as shown below:

```
<button type="button" class="btn btn-primary">Primary</button>
```

The other button classes are:

- btn-default
- btn-primary
- btn-success
- btn-info
- btn-warning
- btn-danger
- btn-link

You can try out some examples of buttons, paired with alert boxes, on the http://www.joyofbootstrap.com website. Just look for the example titled *'Buttons and Alerts'.*

Button Sizes

The following table summarizes classes used to get buttons of various sizes:

Class	Description
.btn-lg	This makes button size large.
.btn-sm	This makes button size small.
.btn-xs	This makes button size with extra small.
.btn-block	This creates block level buttons—those that span the full width of a parent.

Button Groups

Button groups allow you to group a series of buttons together on a single line.

Basic example

Wrap a series of buttons with `.btn` in `.btn-group`.

```
<div class="btn-group">
  <button type="button" class="btn btn-default">Left</button>
  <button type="button" class="btn btn-default">Middle</button>
  <button type="button" class="btn btn-default">Right</button>
</div>
```

Button toolbar

Combine sets of `<div class="btn-group">` into a `<div class="btn-toolbar">` for more complex components.

```
<div class="btn-toolbar" role="toolbar">
  <div class="btn-group">...</div>
  <div class="btn-group">...</div>
  <div class="btn-group">...</div>
```

```
</div>
```

Sizing

Instead of applying button sizing classes to every button in a group, just add `.btn-group-*` to the `.btn-group`.

```
<div class="btn-group btn-group-lg">...</div>
<div class="btn-group">...</div>
<div class="btn-group btn-group-sm">...</div>
<div class="btn-group btn-group-xs">...</div>
```

Nesting Button Groups

Place a `.btn-group` within another `.btn-group` when you want dropdown menus mixed with a series of buttons.

```
<div class="btn-group">
  <button type="button" class="btn btn-default">1</button>
  <button type="button" class="btn btn-default">2</button>

  <div class="btn-group">
    <button type="button" class="btn btn-default dropdown-toggle"
data-toggle="dropdown">
      Dropdown
      <span class="caret"></span>
    </button>
    <ul class="dropdown-menu">
      <li><a href="#">Dropdown link</a></li>
      <li><a href="#">Dropdown link</a></li>
    </ul>
  </div>
</div>
```

Examples

There are several examples of buttons on the http://www.joyofbootstrap.com website, with the category of 'Button'.

Using jQuery with Buttons

Add the optional JavaScript radio and checkbox style behavior with the jQuery button plug in. Note that if you use the default Bootstrap page shown in Chapter two, and include a reference to the **Complete Javascript** library using MaxCDN, you'll already have everything you need to enable this functionality on your page.

Quickstart

Tooltips & popovers in button groups require special setting

When using tooltips or popovers on elements within a `.btn-group`, you'll have to specify the option `container: 'body'` to avoid unwanted side effects (such as the element growing wider and/or losing its rounded corners when the tooltip or popover is triggered).

Sam's Used Cars Challenge

See if you can apply the button feature described in this chapter to Sam's Used Cars website. When you're done, each car on the home page should have a 'buy me' button, something like this:

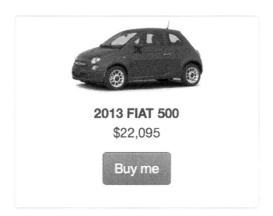

2013 FIAT 500
$22,095

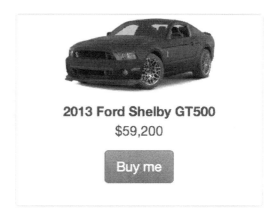

2013 Ford Shelby GT500
$59,200

Challenge Solution

Of course, use your own creativity to come up with how you would set up the site if you were Sam.

One possible solution can be found in the example file Sams_Used_Cars_Chap_10.zip

11

Input Groups

Introduction

Bootstrap allows you to extend form controls by adding text or buttons before, after, or on both sides of any text-based input. This is accomplished by grouping two elements together, such as a plain input box and a currency symbol.

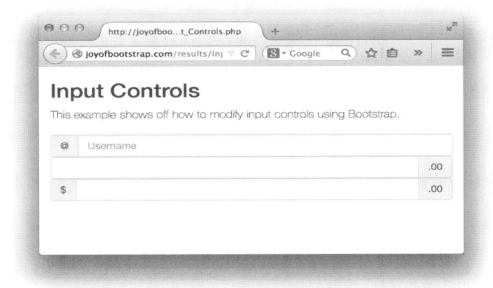

Use the class **input-group** with an .**input-group-addon** to prepend or append elements to a single form-control.

Basic Text Box

Here's an example of a text box with a dollar sign on the left side and two zeroes on the right.   You can add a symbol on either the left or the right, or both, but you cannot add more than one symbol on each side.

```
<div class="input-group">
  <span class="input-group-addon">$</span>
  <input type="text" class="form-control">
  <span class="input-group-addon">.00</span>
</div>
```

Sizing

You can automatically size all the contents of an input group. Just add the relative form sizing classes to the input-group itself and all the contents within that group will automatically size accordingly.

```
<div class="input-group input-group-sm">
  <span class="input-group-addon">@</span>
  <input type="text" class="form-control" placeholder="Username">
</div>
```

The two sizing classes are **input-group-sm** and **input-group-lg**

Other Options

There are other things you can do with input groups too, such as adding a button, radio button, or checkbox next to an input box . However, just because you *can* do something doesn't mean you *should*. I think that these options are more likely to confuse users than help them, so will not cover these features in this book.

Examples

You can try out (and even change) some examples of input groups on the http://www.joyofbootstrap.com website. Just look for the example titled *'Input Group'* and click Try It.

Extra Credit – Amazon.com & Sam's Used Cars

The only place I have seen this used where it actually makes sense is on the Amazon.com search bar.

The drop-down on the left limits the search to specific departments while the button on the right will start the search for the text you type into the input box itself. It's pretty clever but I must admit I usually leave it set to **All Departments** and it still usually finds what I'm looking for.

Could *Sam's Used Cars* use this idea effectively? What would the categories on the left be? One possible solution can be found on www.joyofbootstrap.com as "Input Group with Search Filter"

12

Pagination

Introduction

If you have a web site with lots of article-type pages, or if your site is primarily to provide either news or documentation, then sometimes it makes sense to break up long content across multiple pages.

Of course, splitting an article across multiple pages also helps you serve more ads if your site is ad-funded. You can have a couple of ads on each page and force the user to click across the pages to read the whole article.

Basic Pagination

Bootstrap pagination is super simple. Basically it is just an unordered list with the class of **pagination** added.   Here's some very simple code:

```
<ul class="pagination">
  <li><a href="#">1</a></li>
  <li><a href="#">2</a></li>
  <li><a href="#">3</a></li>
  <li><a href="#">4</a></li>
  <li><a href="#">5</a></li>
</ul>
```

The above code will render as this:

Disabled and active states

It's better for the reader to know which page they are on. Add the class **active** to the list item to indicate the current page by highlighting it.

You may also want to disable a link, although I don't recommend that. Why show a link that's disabled? It doesn't make much sense, but if you insist then add the **disabled** class to the list item.

```
<p>This next set of pagination demonstrates use of a disabled link.
We are on page three, and for some reason page two is disabled.  Is
there a good reason to show disabled links?</p>
<ul class="pagination">
  <li><a
href="http://joyofbootstrap.com/output/simplepagination.php">1</a></
li>
  <li class="disabled"><a href="#">2</a></li>
  <li class="active"><a href="#">3</a></li>
</ul>
```

Sizing

Fancy larger or smaller pagination? Instead of adding the class pagination to the unordered list, instead add either **pagination-lg** or **pagination-sm** for bigger or smaller sizes.

```
<ul class="pagination pagination-lg">...</ul>
<ul class="pagination">...</ul>
<ul class="pagination pagination-sm">...</ul>
```

Alternate Pagination using the Pager

The Pager is a simpler form of pagination, simply providing previous and next links. It's great for simpler sites.

Basic example

By default, the pager centers the links.

```
<ul class="pager">
  <li><a href="#">Previous</a></li>
  <li><a href="#">Next</a></li>
</ul>
```

Aligned links

Alternatively, you can align each link to the sides of the page

```
<ul class="pager">
  <li class="previous"><a href="#"> << Older</a></li>
  <li class="next"><a href="#">Newer >></a></li>
</ul>
```

Examples

The examples from this chapter are available on the http://www.joyofbootstrap.com website.

Chapter 12

Simple Pagination   See Code   View   Download

Advanced Pagination   See Code   View   Download

13

Badges

Introduction to Badges

You have likely never heard the term 'badges' before, but you have surely seen them. Badges are numerical indicators of how many items are associated with a link. For example, at the top of every Kickstarter project is a set of links like this:

Home　　Updates **5**　　Backers **413**　　Comments **10**

The numbers (5, 413, and 10) are the badges. In the case of the first link, the intent is to show that if you click on Updates, you'll be taken to a list of 5 updates.

Bootstrap uses span tags with the class of **badge** to create Badges. We could create this in Bootstrap with the following simple code:

```
<a href="#">Updates <span class="badge">1</span></a>
<a href="#">Backers <span class="badge">387</span></a>
<a href="#">Comments <span class="badge">6</span></a>
```

Using Badges in other Elements

Badge can be used inside other Bootstrap elements, such a buttons and pill boxes.

```
<!-- Badges can be used inside buttons -->
<button type="button" class="btn btn-success">Success <span class="badge">6</span></button>
```

Would produce the following button image:

Examples

There is, of course, an example of using Badges on the http://www.jopyofbootstrap.com website.

14

Jumbotron and Carousel

Introduction

In the real world, a jumbotron is an oversized video screen, typically installed at sports facilities. Here is the jumbotron at Fenway Park in Boston, MA.

In Bootstrap, a jumbotron is a similarly oversized element intended to be a focal point on your web page. Here's a basic example of a jumbotron and how to create it.

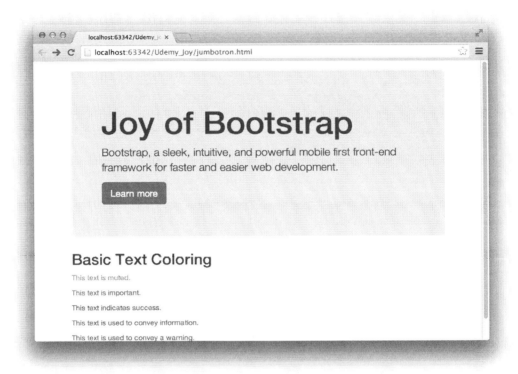

Basic Jumbotron Code

The relevant code that creates the jumbotron shown above is really quite simple:

```
<div class="jumbotron">
   <h1>Joy of Bootstrap</h1>
   <p>Bootstrap, a sleek, intuitive, and powerful mobile first front-end
framework for faster and easier web development.</p>
   <p><a href="http://www.getbootstrap.com" class="btn btn-primary
btn-lg" role="button">Learn more</a></p>
```

```
</div>
```

In the example shown, the jumbotron does not exend to the edge of the screen because it is nested inside a container div (<div class="container">). If you *do* want the jumbotron to extend to the screen edges, don't put it inside a container.

See the section **Containers** in Chapter 2 if you've forgotten about the role the container div plays in sizing and placing Bootstrap elements.

Jumbotron Contents

The contents of the jumbotron appear inside a div with the class of jumbotron

```
<div class="jumbotron">
```

Inside the div you can put nearly any valid HTML, including using other Boostrap elements. In the example above, the following HTML was inside the jumbotron div:

```
1.    <h1>Joy of Bootstrap</h1>
2.       <p>Bootstrap, a sleek, intuitive, and powerful mobile first front-
end framework for faster and easier web development.</p>
3.       <p><a href="http://www.getbootstrap.com" class="btn btn-
primary btn-lg" role="button">Learn more</a></p>
```

Line 1 is an h1 header tag that produces the "headline" Joy of Bootstrap. Line 2 is the paragraph text and line 3 creates the button which is a link to the Bootstrap website. Notice that it is using the Bootstrap button classes.

Jumbotron Example

There is a dedicated example of the Jumbotron that you can try out on the http://www.joyofbootstrap.com website. The specific example can be found here → http://www.joyofbootstrap.com/tryit.php?filename=jumbotron

Jumbotron + jQuery = Carousel

When you combine the idea of a Jumbotron (a big image or billboard) with jQuery (which among other things enables animation) you get the Carousel.

While a Jumbotron displays a single image or message, the Carousel cycles through a number of images or messages, like a slide show.

If you don't know what I mean, you can see an example of a Carousel at http://getbootstrap.com/javascript/#carousel

Of course, because the Carousel is more functional than the Jumbotron, it does take a bit more code to set it up. Quite a bit more. But don't worry-- I'm going to walk you through it and soon you'll understand it just fine.

Carousel Code

Here is the complete code of a page featuring a 4-slide Carousel. Don't worry if you don't understand it all, I didn't either when I first looked at it. In the next section, I'll explain each section.

```
1.    <!DOCTYPE html>
2.    <html lang="en">
3.    <head>
4.      <meta http-equiv="Content-Type" content="text/html; charset=utf-8" />
5.      <title>Joy of Bootstrap – Carousel Example</title>
6.      <script src="//ajax.googleapis.com/ajax/libs/jquery/1.11.1/jquery.min.js"></script>
7.      <link href="//maxcdn.bootstrapcdn.com/bootstrap/3.1.1/css/bootstrap.min.css" rel="stylesheet">
8.      <script src="//maxcdn.bootstrapcdn.com/bootstrap/3.2.0/js/bootstrap.min.js"></script>
9.    </head>
10.   <body>
11.
12.   <div class="container">
13.     <br/>
14.     <div id="carousel-example-generic" class="carousel slide" data-ride="carousel">
15.       <!-- Indicators -->
16.       <ol class="carousel-indicators">
17.         <li data-target="#carousel-example-generic" data-slide-to="0" class="active"></li>
18.         <li data-target="#carousel-example-generic" data-slide-to="1"></li>
19.         <li data-target="#carousel-example-generic" data-slide-to="2"></li>
20.         <li data-target="#carousel-example-generic" data-slide-to="3"></li>
21.       </ol>
22.
23.       <!-- Wrapper for slides -->
24.       <div class="carousel-inner" al>
25.         <div class="item active">
26.           <img src="katahdin_06.jpg" alt="...">
27.           <div class="carousel-caption">
28.             <h3>On the Beach</h3>
29.             <p>Yep, we're close to the ocean.</p>
30.           </div>
31.         </div>
32.         <div class="item">
33.           <img src="katahdin_07.jpg" alt="...">
34.
35.           <div class="carousel-caption">
36.             <h3>Great Location</h3>
37.             <p>The Katahdin Inn is located at the far end of the boardwalk.</p>
38.           </div>
```

```
39.          </div>
40.          <div class="item">
41.            <img src="katahdin_08.jpg" alt="...">
42.            <div class="carousel-caption">
43.              <h3>Short Sands Beach</h3>
44.              <p>Short Sands beach is small and kid friendly.</p>
45.            </div>
46.          </div>
47.
48.          <div class="item">
49.            <div align="center">
50.            <h1>Joy of Bootstrap</h1>
51.            <p>Bootstrap, a sleek, intuitive, and powerful mobile first front-end framework for faster and
easier web development.</p>
52.              <br/>
53.            <p><a href="http://www.getbootstrap.com" class="btn btn-primary btn-lg" role="button">Learn
more</a></p>
54.            </div>
55.          </div>
56.        </div>
57.
58.        <!-- Controls -->
59.        <a class="left carousel-control" href="#carousel-example-generic" role="button" data-slide="prev">
60.          <span class="glyphicon glyphicon-chevron-left"></span>
61.        </a>
62.        <a class="right carousel-control" href="#carousel-example-generic" role="button" data-slide="next">
63.          <span class="glyphicon glyphicon-chevron-right"></span>
64.        </a>
65.      </div>
66.      <h2>Basic Text Coloring</h2>
67.      <p class="text-muted">This text is muted.</p>
68.      <p class="text-primary">This text is important.</p>
69.      <p class="text-success">This text indicates success.</p>
70.      <p class="text-info">This text is used to convey information.</p>
71.      <p class="text-warning">This text is used to convey a warning.</p>
72.      <p class="text-danger">This text is used to convey danger.</p>
73.    </div>
74.  </body>
75.  </html>
```

Code Explained

```
01. <!DOCTYPE html>
02. <html lang="en">
03. <head>
```

```
04.    <meta http-equiv="Content-Type" content="text/html; charset=utf-8" />
05.    <title>Joy of Bootstrap – Carousel Example</title>
06.    <script src="//ajax.googleapis.com/ajax/libs/jquery/1.11.1/jquery.min.js"></script>
07.    <link href="//maxcdn.bootstrapcdn.com/bootstrap/3.1.1/css/bootstrap.min.css" rel="stylesheet">
08.    <script src="//maxcdn.bootstrapcdn.com/bootstrap/3.2.0/js/bootstrap.min.js"></script>
09. </head>
```

Line 1 declares the document as HTML, and **Line 2** declares the language as English.   The rest of the section (the head section) refers to jQuery (**Line 6**) and then Bootstrap (**Lines 7 – 8**).   **Line 10** begins the body section.

```
10.  <body>
11.
12. <div class="container">
13.    <br/>
14.    <div id="carousel-example-generic" class="carousel slide" data-ride="carousel">
15.       <!-- Indicators -->
16.       <ol class="carousel-indicators">
17.          <li data-target="#carousel-example-generic" data-slide-to="0" class="active"></li>
18.          <li data-target="#carousel-example-generic" data-slide-to="1"></li>
19.          <li data-target="#carousel-example-generic" data-slide-to="2"></li>
20.          <li data-target="#carousel-example-generic" data-slide-to="3"></li>
21.       </ol>
```

Line 12 begins a div with the class of container. We've covered this before. The container class centers the content inside it.   **Line 14** begins the div that contains the entire Carousel. This div is closed on **Line 73**. The div has a class of 'carousel slide', which tells Bootstrap that this div contains a carousel. The class data-ride="carousel" tells Bootstrap to begin animating the carousel immediately.

If you leave out the data-ride bit, then the user has to advance the slides manually. Finally, the id='carousel-example-generic' is the name of this particular carousel.   You can call it what you like, but you'll need to use the name consistently as you set up the carousel components; they need to know to which carousel they belong.

Lines 16 - 21 set up the carousel indicators. The indicators are the little dots at the bottom of each slide that indicate to the user how many slides are in the carousel, and which slide they are currently viewing. You can also click on an indicator to jump to that slide.   You need to create one indicator for each slide.

In the image that follows, you see four circles underneath the text. (The text is the caption property, which we'll cover shortly.) The indicators show that this carousel has four slides and that we are currently viewing the third slide.

```
22.
23.    <!-- Wrapper for slides -->
24.    <div class="carousel-inner" >
25.      <div class="item active">
26.        <img src="katahdin_06.jpg" alt="...">
27.        <div class="carousel-caption">
28.          <h3>On the Beach</h3>
29.          <p>Yep, we're close to the ocean.</p>
30.        </div>
31.      </div>
32.      <div class="item">
33.        <img src="katahdin_07.jpg" alt="...">
34.
35.        <div class="carousel-caption">
36.          <h3>Great Location</h3>
37.          <p>The Katahdin Inn is located at the far end of the boardwalk.</p>
38.        </div>
39.      </div>
40.      <div class="item">
```

```
41.          <img src="katahdin_08.jpg" alt="...">
42.          <div class="carousel-caption">
43.            <h3>Short Sands Beach</h3>
44.            <p>Short Sands beach is small and kid friendly.</p>
45.          </div>
46.        </div>
47.
48.        <div class="item">
49.          <div align="center">
50.          <h1>Joy of Bootstrap</h1>
51.          <p>Bootstrap, a sleek, intuitive, and powerful mobile first front-end framework for faster and easier
web development.</p>
52.            <br/>
53.          <p><a href="http://www.getbootstrap.com" class="btn btn-primary btn-lg" role="button">Learn
more</a></p>
54.          </div>
55.        </div>
56.      </div>
57.
```

Lines 24 to 56 are the div that hold the actual slides themselves. This section is created with <div class="carousel-inner" >.

Inside this div is a series of nested divs, one for each slide. The slide is declared with <div class="item"> and you can specify which slide loads first with <div class="item active">.

Within the <div class="item"> you put the content of the slide. This can be text or images, but typically it is an image with a caption. In the blue box that follows is the code that produces the slide that follows;

```
<div class="item">
   <img src="katahdin_08.jpg" alt="picture of beach">
   <div class="carousel-caption">
      <h3>Short Sands Beach</h3>
      <p>Short Sands beach is small and kid friendly.</p>
   </div>
</div>
```

```
58.     <!-- Controls -->
59.     <a class="left carousel-control" href="#carousel-example-generic" role="button" data-slide="prev">
60.         <span class="glyphicon glyphicon-chevron-left"></span>
61.     </a>
62.     <a class="right carousel-control" href="#carousel-example-generic" role="button" data-slide="next">
63.         <span class="glyphicon glyphicon-chevron-right"></span>
64.     </a>
65. </div>
```

Finally, we need to add the code that creates the left and right buttons that allow the user to go back and forth between the slides manually. **Lines 59 – 64** create these controls.

Notice that the images < and > are glyphicons, which are covered in an earlier chapter.

Line 65 closes the Carousel div we started with the line <div id="carousel-example-generic" class="carousel slide" data-ride="carousel">

The rest of the page is just some basic HTML so that the carousel is not the only thing on the page. **Line 73** closes the container div.

```
66.     <h2>Basic Text Coloring</h2>
67.     <p class="text-muted">This text is muted.</p>
68.     <p class="text-primary">This text is important.</p>
69.     <p class="text-success">This text indicates success.</p>
70.     <p class="text-info">This text is used to convey information.</p>
71.     <p class="text-warning">This text is used to convey a warning.</p>
72.     <p class="text-danger">This text is used to convey danger.</p>
73. </div>
74. </body>
75. </html>
```

Adding Captions

As noted above, captions are added to a slide by adding a div as follows, inside the item div.

```
<div class="carousel-caption">
        <h3>Short Sands Beach</h3>
        <p>Short Sands beach is small and kid friendly.</p>
</div>
```

Carousel Quirks

The Bootstrap Carousel is not without its flaws. You may notice that the fourth slide in the example above does not have an image associated with it. When the user gets to that slide, the Carousel will resize because the content of slide 4 doesn't require as much space as the other slides. This will also occur if the images are not all the same size.

Another quirk is that if the images are not as wide as the carousel, Bootstrap left aligns the image, which in my opinion looks dumb.

An Improved Carousel

In researching this book I found a number of attempts at addressing the Carousel's limitations, and the best one I found was at:

http://parkhurstdesign.com/improved-carousels-twitter-bootstrap/

I won't go into detail at the solution but if you want to find it yourself, do a search for "Twitter Bootstrap Improved Carousels" and you'll soon find it.

15

Page Headers

Introduction

This could be the shortest chapter ever written. Bootstrap has something called a page header. According to the Bootstrap documentation, a page header is simple shell for an h1 to appropriately space out and segment sections of content on a page. What does that mean exactly?

I experimented a bit to see if I could find out. As near as I could tell, the page header is really more like a section divider. When you use the page header you get a nice horizontal line under the div you create.

Sample Code

To use the Page Header element, create a div with the class of 'page-header' as shown:

```
<div class="page-header">
  <h1>Example page header <small>Subtext for header</small></h1>
</div>
```

Example

See the www.joyofbootstrap.com website for an example. You can also go directly to http://www.joyofbootstrap.com/tryit.php?filename=pageheader

16

Images

Responsive Images

Images come in all sizes. So do screens. Wouldn't it be great if you could automatically adjust an image to fit the size of the screen the user is using to view the image? Yes, that would be great, and Bootstrap makes this very easy.

To match up the size of the image to the available screen size, just add the class `class="img-responsive"` to a standard image tag.

You can see an example of this on the website at http://www.joyofbootstrap.com/tryit.php?filename=responsiveimages

Image Shapes (Squares and Circles)

Bootstrap also allows you to manipulate images so that they appear inside shapes. This is super easy to do. Simply add one of the image classes to a standard image tag.   Consider the following code snippet:

```
<h1>Image Shapes</h1>
<p class="lead">This image will automatically appear inside a circle.
Other options are img-rounded and img-square. </p>
<img src="/images/surfer.jpg" class="img-circle" width="25%"
height="25%" alt="Surfer Dude">
```

The bit of code highlighted in yellow is the part that matters. The above code, on a page with the appropriate Bootstrap framework would produce the following page:

Image Shapes

This image will automatically appear inside a circle. Other options are img-rounded and img-square.

The image shape options are circle, square, and rounded square, as follows:

1. img-circle

2. img-rounded

3. img-square

Image Thumbnails

Used in conjunction with Bootstrap's grid system you can use Bootstrap's thumbnail component to produce nice grids of image thumbnails with or without explanatory text.

I struggled a bit with this one. The official Bootstrap documentation offers very little explanation of how this works, and their example uses `img data-src=` (which calls a javascript function you cannot get to) rather than `img src=` to define their images. I don't know *why* they did it that way, but if you actually want to display an image, you need to use the `img src=` format.

Eventually I got it to work, and you can find (and modify) the example at

http://www.joyofbootstrap.com/tryit.php?filename=imagethumbnails

Image Thumbnail Sample Code

```
01.  <!DOCTYPE html>
02.  <html lang="en">
03.  <head>
04.  <meta http-equiv="Content-Type" content="text/html; charset=utf-8" />
05.  <title></title>
06.   <!-- Bootstrap -->
07.   <!-- Latest compiled and minified CSS -->
08.  <link
href="//maxcdn.bootstrapcdn.com/bootstrap/3.1.1/css/bootstrap.min.css" rel="stylesheet">
09.  </head>
10.   <body>
11.  <div class="container">
12.  <h1 class="page-header">Image Thumbnails <small>without much work</small></h1>
13.  <p class="lead">Image thumbnails are a great way to display a gallery of images. Users can click the image to see it full size.</p>
14.  <div class="container-fluid">
15.   <div class="row">
16.   <div class="col-xs-6 col-md-3">
17.    <a href="/images/surfer.jpg" class="thumbnail">
18.    <img src="/images/surfer.jpg" alt="surfer">
19.    </a>
20.   </div>
21.  <div class="col-xs-6 col-md-3">
22.    <a href="/images/nubble.jpg" class="thumbnail">
23.    <img src="/images/nubble.jpg" alt="Nubble lighthouse">
```

```
24.    </a>
25. <h3>Nubble Light</h3>
26.    <p>America's most photographed lighthouse.</p>
27.  </div>
28. <div class="col-xs-6 col-md-3">
29.   <a href="/images/petit.jpg" class="thumbnail">
30.    <img src="/images/petit.jpg" alt="Le Petit Palais in Nice,
FR">
31. <h3>Hotel du Petit Palais</h3>
32.    <p>Nestled in the hills overlooking Nice FR</p>
33.   </a>
34.  </div>
35. </div>
36.  </div>
37.  </body>
38. </html>
```

Lines 1 – 13 should be familiar to you know. They simply set up the basic page and add the Bootstrap components.

The lines that make the individual thumbnails are inside a div defining a grid row.   An individual thumbnail is created in **Lines 16 – 20** and looks like this:

```
<div class="row">
```

```
16.   <div class="col-xs-6 col-md-3">
17.   <a href="/images/surfer.jpg" class="thumbnail">
18.    <img src="/images/surfer.jpg" alt="surfer">
19.   </a>
20.   </div>
```

```
</div>
```

If you want to have an explanation of the image underneath it, you can add markup inside the div a shown in **Lines 21 – 27.**

```
21. <div class="col-xs-6 col-md-3">
22.    <a href="/images/nubble.jpg" class="thumbnail">
```

```
23.    <img src="/images/nubble.jpg" alt="Nubble lighthouse">
24.    </a>
25. <h3>Nubble Light</h3>
26.    <p>America's most photographed lighthouse.</p>
27.    </div>
```

Finally, depending on whether you want the explanatory text to be clickable or not, you simply include your text inside the anchor tag or not. In the above example **(Lines 21 – 27)** only the image is clickable.

In the below example, **(Lines 28 – 34)** the user can click on either the image or the text.

```
28. <div class="col-xs-6 col-md-3">
29.    <a href="/images/petit.jpg" class="thumbnail">
30.    <img src="/images/petit.jpg" alt="Le Petit Palais in Nice, FR">
31. <h3>Hotel du Petit Palais</h3>
32.    <p>Nestled in the hills overlooking Nice FR</p>
33.    </a>
34.    </div>
```

Sample Code

The companion website http://www.joyofbootstrap.com has several examples of Bootstrap image manipulation.   Simply search for 'image' to locate them.

Chapter 16

Image With Captions	See Code	View	Download
Responsive Images	See Code	View	Download
Image Shapes	See Code	View	Download
Image Thumbnails	See Code	View	Download

17

Progress Bars

Introduction

Progress Bars are great for showing the user how far along they are in a process, or how far along an operation has proceeded. Bootstrap provides for a variety of styles, starting with the basic bar, shown below:

Basic Progress Bar

Progress Bar with value displayed

60%

Basic Progress Bar

A basic progress bar is made with the following code:

```
<div class="progress">
 <div class="progress-bar" role="progressbar" aria-valuenow="50" aria-valuemin="0" aria-valuemax="100" style="width: 50%;">
  <span class="sr-only">50% Complete</span>
```

```
</div>
</div>
```

The first div is <div class="progress"> which is the container for the progress bar. Next you put values inside this div by adding items such as:

```
<div class="progress-bar" role="progressbar" aria-valuenow="50" aria-
valuemin="0" aria-valuemax="100" style="width: 50%;">
```

Why two nested divs? Because as you'll see in the next section, you can create stacked bars by nesting the inner divs inside a single <div class="progress"> div.

Finally, create the span which will hold the progress bar with something like this:

```
<span class="sr-only">50% Complete</span>
```

Whether the text inside the span is displayed or not depends on whether you use the class 'sr-only'. If that class is applied, then only a plain bar will display, and if you remove it, the text inside the span will appear inside the bar.

The best way to understand how all these pieces work together is to experiment with the examples on the http://www.joyofbootstrap.com web site. The basic progress bar example can be found at:

http://www.joyofbootstrap.com/tryit.php?filename=progressbars

Advanced Progress Bars

There are some other things you can do with progress bars too. You can colorize them with the standard info, warning, and danger classes with the following code:

```
<div class="progress">
 <div class="progress-bar progress-bar-warning" role="progressbar"
aria-valuenow="60" aria-valuemin="0" aria-valuemax="100" style="width:
```

```
60%">
 <span class="sr-only">60% Complete (warning)</span>
 </div>
</div>
```

The change from the earlier version is adding the class progress-bar-warning.

Other valid classes include:

progress-bar-warning

progress-bar-success

progress-bar-info

progress-bar-danger

Examples of colorized progress bars are shown below:

Progress Bars using Bootstrap Colors

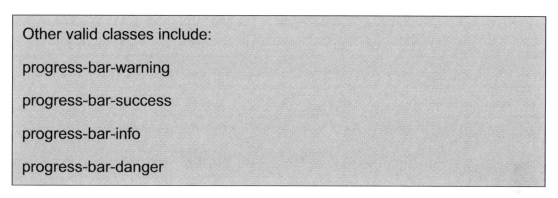

You can try out the colorized examples here →
http://www.joyofbootstrap.com/tryit.php?
filename=progressbarsusingbootstrapcolors

Stacked Bars

Progress bars can be stacked by including more than one progress-bar div inside the parent <div class='progress'> div, as shown:

```
Drive C:
<div class="progress">
 <div class="progress-bar progress-bar-success" style="width: 35%">
  <span>Free Space</span>
 </div>

 <div class="progress-bar progress-bar-danger" style="width: 10%">
  <span class="sr-only">10% Complete (danger)</span>
 </div>
</div>

Drive D:
 <div class="progress">

 <div class="progress-bar progress-bar-success" style="width: 55%">
  <span>Free Space</span>
 </div>

 <div class="progress-bar progress-bar-danger" style="width: 8%">
  <span >10%</span>
 </div>
 </div>
</div>
```

The above code would render as:

Stacked Progress Bars using Bootstrap Colors

Drive C:

Drive D:

Exercise

Go to the website and experiment with where you place the drive name and other attributes to understand how this goes together. The example can be found at:

http://www.joyofbootstrap.com/tryit.php?filename=stackedbarprogressbars

18

Media Objects

Introduction

Bootstrap has a component it calls "media object". I don' t know about you, but when I think of media I think of embedded video or audio. This is **not** what the media object component is about.

The *Bootstrap* media object is a way of grouping images and text in a way that looks nice. Here's an example:

Surfer Dude 1

The suave surfer dude always catches the eyes of the ladies.

Surfer Dude 2

Of course, sometimes the ladies catch the attention of the surfer dude.

According to the Bootstrap documentation, you can use this component to organize tweets, blog comments, and other such text alongside a left or right aligned image.

Media Object Code

To create a media object, use the code similar to the following:

```
<div class="media">
 <a class="pull-left" href="#">
  <img class="media-object" src="/images/surfer.jpg" height=64px
width=64px alt="surfer">
 </a>
 <div class="media-body">
  <h4 class="media-heading">Surfer Dude 1</h4>
  The suave surfer dude always catches the eyes of the ladies. </div>
</div>
```

First, create a div with the class of "media". Within the media div, you can create any number of rows. Each row has two components: an image and a body. The image is created with the class "media-object" while the text appears inside its own div with the class of "media-body". Finally, within the media-body div you can also set the headline to have the "media-heading" class.

Sample Media Object Code

You can find a complete sample media object you can experiment with on the www.joyofbootstrap.com website. The example can be found directly at: http://www.joyofbootstrap.com/tryit.php?filename=basicmediaobject

19

List Groups

Introduction

List groups are pretty simple. Basically they are an element with a box around it, or a group of elements with each element in a box.

The most basic list group is a variation of the unordered list. Consider a basic list:

```
<ul>
    <li>First item</li>
    <li>Second item</li>
    <li>Third item</li>
</ul>
```

Adding a couple of Bootstrap classes transforms it into a list group:

```
<ul class="list-group">
  <li class="list-group-item">First item</li>
  <li class="list-group-item">Second item</li>
  <li class="list-group-item">Third item</li>
</ul>
```

It will look like this:

Badges in List Groups

You can easily add badges to a list group by creating a span with the badge class.   Recall that badges were covered in chapter 13.

```
<ul class="list-group">
  <li class="list-group-item">
    <span class="badge">14</span>
    Alerts
  </li>
</ul>
```

List Groups of Links

The list-group class can also be applied to divs which contain links. In this case, you will follow the same basic pattern as the basic example (the parent item has the class "list-group" while the items have the class "list-group-item".

The following is an example:

```
<div class="list-group">
   <a href="#" class="list-group-item active">
     First Item - Active
   </a>
   <a href="#" class="list-group-item">Second Item</a>
   <a href="#" class="list-group-item">Third Item</a>
</div>
```

Colorful List Groups

Bootstrap has a consistent method for setting common colors across all its components. By now you are (hopefully) familiar with the notion of 'info', 'danger', and 'success' classes. This standard also applies to list groups.

To colorize a list-group item, use the following classes:

```
<div class="list-group">
   <a href="#" class="list-group-item list-group-item-success">Success</a>
   <a href="#" class="list-group-item list-group-item-info">Information</a>
   <a href="#" class="list-group-item list-group-item-warning">Warning</a>
   <a href="#" class="list-group-item list-group-item-danger">Danger</a>
</div>
```

Complex List Group Items

List group items are not limited to simple list items or link tags. Nearly any HTML can go inside a list group item. Bootstrap also provides the convenient classes "list-group-item-heading" and "list-group-item-text" which can be used as follows:

```
<div class="list-group">
   <a href="#" class="list-group-item active">
      <h4 class="list-group-item-heading">Attention</h4>
      <p class="list-group-item-text">Please be sure to wash your hands before returning to
work.</p>
   </a>
</div>
```

renders as:

Attention
Please be sure to wash your hands before returning to work.

20

Panels and Wells

Introduction

To help make certain content stand out on a page, you can put it inside a panel or a well.   A panel is simply a box with lines and padding; a well is basically the same thing except the lines have a bit more styling to make it seem as if they are set into the page. Here's a basic panel:

Basic panel example, with class of panel-success

Panels have more options and seem to be more flexible than wells.

The Basic Panel

A panel is created by creating a div and giving it the class 'panel' followed by one of the style directives, such as **'panel-default'**

```
<div class="panel panel-default">
  <div class="panel-body">
    Basic panel example
  </div>
</div>
```

Panel Classes

Other valid panel directives include:

1. <div class="panel panel-primary">

2. <div class="panel panel-success">

3. <div class="panel panel-info">

4. <div class="panel panel-warning">

5. <div class="panel panel-danger">

Declaring one of the panel directives such as panel-warning changes the color of the line surrounding the panel.

Panel Headers and Footers

Panels can have headers and footers, and those headers and footers can contain h1 - h6 tags within them.   The basic idea is to create a div with the class of panel-heading or panel-footer inside the parent panel div. As with the basic example, the panel content goes inside a div with the panel-body class.

Headers

Here is a code example

```
<div class="panel panel-warning">
  <div class="panel-heading">
     <h3 class="panel-title">H3 Panel Title - Warning</h3>
  </div>
 <div class="panel-body">
  Hey, you should really pay attention to what's inside this box.
</div>
</div>
```

Plain panel heading - Info

Easily add a heading container to your panel with .panel-heading. You may also include any head tags with a .panel-title class to add a pre-styled heading.

For proper link coloring, be sure to place links in headings within .panel-title.

H3 Panel Title - Warning

Hey, you should really pay attention to what's inside this box.

Footers

Footers can be created in the same basic way; within the panel div, add a div with the class of panel-footer, as shown:

```
<div class="panel panel-default">
  <div class="panel-body">
    Panel content
  </div>
  <div class="panel-footer">Panel footer</div>
</div>
```

Wells

Wells seem to have fewer options than Panels. I played around with mixing and matching some of the classes that are associated with panels and found that some of the classes I thought would work in Wells do not. Oh well!

Basic Well

The basic well is created by making a well with the class of well, such as
`<div class="well">...</div>`

Well Classes

As far as I could discover, the only classes suitable for use with wells are small and large, represented as:

1. `<div class="well well-lg">...</div>`

2. `<div class="well well-sm">...</div>`

21

Bootstrap and JavaScript Together

Introduction

JavaScript is the primary language used for scripting objects in the browser, particularly when it comes to animation. So it naturally follows that the Bootstrap elements that include animation or action (such as drop-downs, transitions, color changes, etc.) are really using JavaScript to accomplish their effect.

Both `bootstrap.js` and `bootstrap.min.js` contain all plugins in a single file. You only need to include one or the other. Bootstrap.js is readable by humans, but the longer of the two. Bootstrap.min.js is a minified version of the same file, which makes it smaller, but also unreadable except to computers. When in doubt, use the minified version.

Anytime you are using a Bootstrap component that requires JavaScript, simply include the following line near the top of your page:

```
<script
src="http://netdna.bootstrapcdn.com/bootstrap/3.1.1/js/bootstrap.min.js">
</script>
```

If you are working with a Bootstrap component and it isn't working the way you expect, one likely cause is that the page doesn't have the JavaScript it needs. I have fallen into that trap more than once.

jQuery

In case you haven't heard of it, jQuery is a JavaScript library which exists to make working with JavaScript easier. Bootstrap and jQuery work well together, and it seems that the developers of Bootstrap decided to use jQuery wherever JavaScript was required.

If you haven't encountered jQuery before, I recommend my book *"The Joy of jQuery"* which is available in Kindle and Paperback formats on Amazon.

If you are already familiar with jQuery, you are in luck because you can leverage that knowledge with Bootstrap.

22

jQuery Tabs

Introduction

Tabs are a great way of fitting lots of content onto a page at once, without overwhelming the user. The tab control shows categories of information along the top (usually, but other orientations are possible) and the user can select the content they are most interested in.

For instance, Sam's Used Cars might use tabs on a page dedicated to a specific vehicle, as shown below:

Overview	Photograph	Financing

Nissan Pathfinder

Body Style: Sport Utility

Exterior Color: Red / Brown

Fuel: Gasoline

Transmission: 5-Speed Automatic

Users can see an overview of the car, switch to see a photograph, or find out how much the car costs.

You can see the full example and grab the code here →
http://joyofbootstrap.com/tryit.php?filename=basictabcontrol

Tab Code

```
01. <!DOCTYPE html>
02. <html lang="en">
03. <head>
04. <meta http-equiv="Content-Type" content="text/html; charset=utf-8" />
05. <title>A Basic Bootstrap Tab Page</title>
06.    <!-- Bootstrap -->
07.    <!-- Latest compiled and minified CSS -->
08. <link href="//maxcdn.bootstrapcdn.com/bootstrap/3.1.1/css/bootstrap.min.css"
rel="stylesheet">
09.    <script src="https://ajax.googleapis.com/ajax/libs/jquery/1.11.0/jquery.min.js"></script>
10. <script src="//maxcdn.bootstrapcdn.com/bootstrap/3.1.1/js/bootstrap.min.js"></script>
11. </head>
12.    <body>
13. <div class="container">
14. <h1  class="page-header">Sam's Used Cars <small>2008 Nissan
Pathfinder</small></h1>
15. <p class="lead">Tabs are a great way to fit a lot of content on the page at once, without
seeming overwhelming at first.</p>
16. <!-- Nav tabs -->
17. <ul class="nav nav-tabs" role="tablist">
18.    <li class="active"><a href="#overview" role="tab" data-toggle="tab">Overview</a></li>
19.    <li><a href="#photos" role="tab" data-toggle="tab">Photograph</a></li>
20.    <li><a href="#financing" role="tab" data-toggle="tab">Financing</a></li>
21. </ul>
22.
23. <!-- Tab panes -->
24. <div class="tab-content">
25. <div class="tab-pane active" id="overview">
26.    <h2>Nissan Pathfinder</h2>
27.    Body Style: Sport Utility <br/>
28.    Exterior Color: Red / Brown <br/>
29.    Fuel: Gasoline <br/>
30.    Transmission: 5-Speed Automatic <br/>
31.    Drivetrain: 4WD<br/>
32.    Doors: 4<br/>
33.    Engine:  4.0L V6 24V <br/>
34.    </div>
```

```
35.
36.   <div class="tab-pane" id="photos">
37.      <a href="/images/nissan.jpg" class="thumbnail">
38.      <img src="/images/nissan.jpg" alt="Nissan Pathfinder">
39.      </a>
40.  </div>
41.
42.   <div class="tab-pane" id="financing">
43.  <h2>No money, no worries!</h2>
44.     Don't worry, everybody gets financing at Sam's Used Cars.
45.   </div>
46.
47.  </div>
48.  </div>
49.   </body>
50.  </html>
```

Code Explained

Page Prerequisites

Lines 1 – 11 set up the basic prerequisites that enable to the page to work:

```
01.  <!DOCTYPE html>
02.  <html lang="en">
03.  <head>
04.  <meta http-equiv="Content-Type" content="text/html; charset=utf-8" />
05.  <title>A Basic Bootstrap Tab Page</title>
06.     <!-- Bootstrap -->
07.     <!-- Latest compiled and minified CSS -->
08.  <link href="//maxcdn.bootstrapcdn.com/bootstrap/3.1.1/css/bootstrap.min.css" rel="stylesheet">
09.     <script src="https://ajax.googleapis.com/ajax/libs/jquery/1.11.0/jquery.min.js"></script>
10.  <script src="//maxcdn.bootstrapcdn.com/bootstrap/3.1.1/js/bootstrap.min.js"></script>
11.  </head>
```

Line 3 opens the <head> section of the page and **Line 11** closes it. Line 8 is a link to the hosted Bootstrap CSS file. **Line 9** is a link to the hosted jQuery file. jQuery is required to enable the (limited) animation provided by the tab control. When you click on a tab, the content of the selected tab is revealed while the prior tab's content is hidden. **Line 10** is a link to the Bootstrap Javascript file. Without all three of these references, the page will not work.

```
13. <div class="container">
14. <h1 class="page-header">Sam's Used Cars <small>2008 Nissan
Pathfinder</small></h1>
15. <p class="lead">Tabs are a great way to fit a lot of content on the page at once, without
seeming overwhelming at first.</p>
```

Line 13 is a DIV with the class of container. Adding this DIV to a page makes it center and generally look better. This DIV is closed on **Line 49**.

Line 14 produces a page header at the top of the page, and **Line 15** creates the text starting with "Tabs are a great way..." as shown below:

Sam's Used Cars 2008 Nissan Pathfinder

Tabs are a great way to fit a lot of content on the page at once, without seeming overwhelming at first.

| Overview | Photograph | Financing |

Tab Control

We begin setting up the tabs with **Line 16** which is a comment that will make the code easier to read later. Comments are **always** a good idea.

```
16.  <!-- Nav tabs -->
17.  <ul class="nav nav-tabs" role="tablist">
18.    <li class="active"><a href="#overview" role="tab" data-toggle="tab">Overview</a></li>
19.    <li><a href="#photos" role="tab" data-toggle="tab">Photograph</a></li>
20.    <li><a href="#financing" role="tab" data-toggle="tab">Financing</a></li>
21.  </ul>
```

The tab effect is created by Bootstrap by adding custom styling to an unordered list. Bootstrap knows which unordered lists to transform into a tab control because of the class (nav nav-tabs) and role (tablist) attributes added to the list.

Our tab control will have three tabs so our unordered list will have three list items. The list begins on **Line 17** and ends on **Line 21**. Within our unordered list we have three list items, one for each tab. They are created on **Lines 18, 19, and 20**. Note that each list item contains a link (<a href=) tag to a specific div (the #name). These list items also have a Bootstrap-specific role (tab) and data-toggle attributes.

Tab Content

Next we'll set up the content that goes inside each tab. All the tab content goes inside a single div with the class of tab-content. The tab-content div starts on **Line 24** and is closed on **Line 48**.

```
23.  <!-- Tab panes -->
24.  <div class="tab-content">
25.    <div class="tab-pane active" id="overview">
26.      <h2>Nissan Pathfinder</h2>
27.      Body Style: Sport Utility <br/>
28.      Exterior Color: Red / Brown <br/>
29.      Fuel: Gasoline <br/>
30.      Transmission: 5-Speed Automatic <br/>
31.      Drivetrain: 4WD<br/>
32.      Doors: 4<br/>
33.      Engine:  4.0L V6 24V <br/>
```

```
34.   </div>
35.
36.   <div class="tab-pane" id="photos">
37.      <a href="/images/nissan.jpg" class="thumbnail">
38.      <img src="/images/nissan.jpg" alt="Nissan Pathfinder">
39.      </a>
40.  </div>
```

The content for the first pane ("Overview") is defined between Lines 25 and Line 40, shown above.

The content of each tab is defined with a div with an ID that matches the link tag. In the case of the Overview tab, the link to this content is defined on Line 18 (repeated below). Notice that the href tag in **Line 18** refers to #overview and that the div defined on **Line 25** has the id of "overview". This is how the tab and its content are linked.

```
18.    <li class="active"><a href="#overview" role="tab" data-toggle="tab">Overview</a></li>
...
25.    <div class="tab-pane active" id="overview">
```

Every div has the same class of tab-pane but each div must have a unique id. The careful reader might notice that the first tab (**Line 25**) has an additional attribute for the div – active. Adding this attribute to the div makes the tab content visible when the page first loads. Only one tab should be active, and it should match the tab content that is active.

Notice that both **Line 18** and **Line 25** are marked active, albeit in different ways. The actual tab content – what you see when you click on a tab – is what comes next in Lines 26 – 33.

```
26.    <h2>Nissan Pathfinder</h2>
27.    Body Style: Sport Utility <br/>
28.    Exterior Color: Red / Brown <br/>
29.    Fuel: Gasoline <br/>
30.    Transmission: 5-Speed Automatic <br/>
31.    Drivetrain: 4WD<br/>
32.    Doors: 4<br/>
33.    Engine:  4.0L V6 24V <br/>
```

The HTML inside the tab is just ordinary HTML. As near as I could tell, any HTML can go inside a tab's content.

Our next tab, the photograph tab, takes just 5 lines to create.

```
36.    <div class="tab-pane" id="photos">
37.        <a href="/images/nissan.jpg" class="thumbnail">
38.        <img src="/images/nissan.jpg" alt="Nissan Pathfinder">
39.      </a>
40.  </div>
```

Line 36 starts the div with the class of "tab-pane" (same as the previous tab) and an id of "photos" (this id is unique). Inside this div is an anchor tag with the class of "thumbnail". Recall from Chapter 16 that this class attribute makes the image responsive-- meaning it will fill to the available space in the tab, which is quite cool.

Line 40 closes this div and finishes all that is required for our second tab. The third tab works the same way, and I'm sure you'll figure it out.

Use the example at ..

http://joyofbootstrap.com/tryit.php?filename=basictabcontrol

… as a starting point for your experimentation. See if you can add a new tab or change the content inside the tabs to something different.

23

jQuery Tooltips and Popovers

Introduction

Tooltips and popovers provide a way to provide additional information to your user when they need it. For example, you can show a tooltip when a user mouses over a button or link.

In the example shown below, the tooltip is shown below the button. While the screen shot doesn't capture it, the tooltip only appears because my mouse is over the button.

Tooltip test

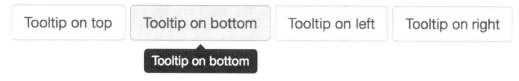

Tooltips vs Popovers: What's the difference?

The difference between a tooltip and a popover, at least as far as Bootstrap is concerned, is how much information each can show. A tooltip contains a single line of information, and cannot contain any markup. A popover is slightly more sophisticated in that it has a title, can span multiple lines, and has a few more options.

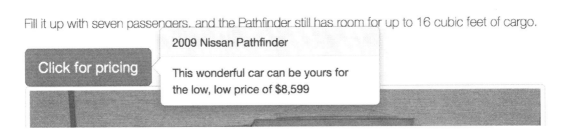

Creating a Tooltip

If you take a look at the Bootstrap documentation, it looks as if creating a tooltip is super easy.

```
<button type="button" class="btn btn-default" data-toggle="tooltip" data-placement="top" title="Tooltip on top">Tooltip on top</button>
```

Simply create a button and add a few extra parameters and you're all set, right? Well, I tried that and my tooltip didn't work. It isn't well explained but you also need to put a jQuery function in the document load (ready) event.

The following code needs to go in the head section for it to work:

```
<script>
  $(document).ready(function() {
  $("body").tooltip({ selector: '[data-toggle=tooltip]' });
});
  </script>
```

Find an example at http://joyofbootstrap.com/tryit.php?filename=basictooltip

Creating a Popover

A popover is created in basically the same way:

```
<button type="button" class="btn btn-lg btn-info" data-toggle="popover" title="2009 Nissan Pathfinder" data-content="This wonderful car can be yours for the low, low price of $8,599">Click for pricing</button>
```

By looking at it you can pretty much figure out the various attributes you can set (such as btn-danger instead of btn-info).

The following code needs to go in the document head section for it to work:

```
<script>
  $(document).ready(function() {
  $("body").popover({ selector: '[data-toggle=popover]' });
});
  </script>
```

You can find an example of a popover at http://joyofbootstrap.com/tryit.php?filename=basicpopover

24

Conclusion

Wrapping it up

I hope by now you have gotten a good sense of the power of Bootstrap. Did this book cover everything there is to know about Bootstrap? I wish it were possible.

Bootstrap is a very rich topic and it is always improving and evolving. So a book about it could never be complete. I do hope you have gotten enough to be successful with it though.

Internet Resources

Be sure to check out these great resources:

http://www.joyofbootstrap.com

http://getbootstrap.com/

For Bootstrap themes and templates: http://startbootstrap.com/

Bootstrap themes: http://bootswatch.com/

Books by the same Author

Did you like this book? If so you might like other books by the same author. Look on Amazon.com for

- The Joy of PHP

- The Joy of jQuery

Printed in Great Britain
by Amazon